A souvenir guide

Lacock
Wiltshire

National Trust

Lacock's Long History

In the early 13th century Ela, Countess of Salisbury, established a nunnery by the River Avon at Lacock. The abbey and village have been interlinked ever since.

The stones of Lacock tell numerous stories stretching back almost 800 years. The abbey is one of the most complete surviving medieval nunneries in Britain. This is a rare survival as, after 300 years of religious life, the nuns were forced to abandon the abbey during the Dissolution of the Monasteries in 1539. The convent became a country house as the Sharington and Talbot families made it their home, with more than a nod to the abbey's medieval and religious origins.

Lacock Abbey is also famous as the birthplace of an invention that changed the way we see the world. Here William Henry Fox Talbot developed the photographic negative process: you can see the window immortalised in the world's first negative, made in 1835, and his invention is celebrated in the Fox Talbot Museum at the abbey gates.

Given the part played by the abbey in the invention of photography, it is fitting that Lacock is now famous as a film location. Filmmakers have been drawn here by the village's unspoilt character, where you will feel for yourself that the past is very much present.

The Dissolution of the Monasteries
Henry VIII targeted monasteries after he broke with Rome and the Catholic Church to divorce Catherine of Aragon in 1533. Religious orders had become wealthy landowners and the king resolved to suppress them following the establishment of his new Church of England. A national audit in 1535–36 identified poorly run houses but Lacock Abbey survived until the final wave of closures in 1539.

Left Over 800 years of history including a world-famous invention make Lacock a fascinating visit

Right Church Street, one of four making up the village's grid plan

A brief history

The story begins with Ela, Countess of Salisbury, the powerful and well-connected woman who became Lacock's first abbess. The abbey buildings were built in the 1200s, and altered in the 1300s and 1400s. Then came William Sharington (see page 25), the ambitious Tudor courtier who converted the abbey into his home from 1540, adding some of the earliest Renaissance-inspired architecture in Britain. In the 18th century, John Ivory Talbot made major changes to the garden and turned the abbey into an important monument of the Gothick Revival that occurred in the Georgian period. William Henry Fox Talbot made further alterations and about 1830 added the projecting Gothic-style oriel windows (an oriel window is a form of bay window that projects from the main wall of a building but does not reach to the ground). His son Charles carried out some careful restoration, and it was Charles's niece Matilda who gave Lacock to the National Trust.

From Sharington to Talbot

Lacock Abbey and village have been in the National Trust's care since 1944. They owe their remarkable preservation to a lack of development after the early 1800s and owners who understood the historic value of their inheritance.

William Sharington (c.1495–1553) transformed the abbey buildings from a convent into a country house but only lived here for 13 years before his death. Not one of his three marriages produced children, so the estate passed to his younger brother Henry (died 1581), who was knighted by Queen Elizabeth I during her visit to Lacock in September 1574. Sir Henry willed the property to his youngest daughter Olive (died

Seconds out
In 1668 Sir John Talbot was wounded in one of the most famous duels in British history, acting as second to his Talbot cousin, the Earl of Shrewsbury, who was killed by the Duke of Buckingham. Seconds were assistants and arbiters, whose duties included reconciliation in the first instance but also loading the weapons and setting the time and terms of firing. Sir John's son, Sharington, also died as the result of a duel, in 1685.

1646). She married John Talbot of Salwarp (now Salwarpe) in Worcestershire, a descendant of Lacock Abbey's founder Ela. Olive's son Sharington Talbot died four years before her in 1642, so the next to succeed was her grandson Sharington Talbot the Younger (died 1677).

Left William Sharington was an ambitious man whose connections with the family of Henry VIII's third queen, Jane Seymour, helped him accumulate a large estate

Fighters for a cause
During the Civil War the Talbots supported King Charles I. Their home became a Royalist garrison until, in 1645, Bristol and Devizes fell to Parliamentary forces and Sharington was forced to surrender the abbey. His younger brother, Gilbert, was thrown into Gloucester jail for plotting the return of Charles II. When Charles II was restored to the throne in 1660, Gilbert was elected a founder member of the Royal Society, 'a Colledge for the Promoting of Physico-Mathematicall Experimentall Learning'. He ended his days at Lacock, which in 1677 became the property of his nephew Sir John Talbot (1630–1714).

Lacock's Long History

Above William Henry Fox Talbot, the Victorian pioneer of photography and inventor of the negative

Top right Matilda Talbot, cookery teacher, traveller and the last member of the Talbot family to own Lacock Abbey; painted by Lord Methuen, RA (1886–1974)

Later Talbots

John Ivory (1691?–1772), Sir John's eldest grandson by his second wife, inherited in 1714 and added the Talbot name to his own. His 58 years as owner dramatically altered the look of Lacock but the next three owners had far shorter tenures. Ivory Talbot's son John (1717?–78) died childless, six years after inheriting. Lacock then passed to his sister Martha (died 1790), who had married her cousin the Reverend William Davenport. Theirs was the third Talbot-Davenport match, which explains the number of Davenport portraits in the house.

In 1790 the estate passed to Martha's son, William Davenport Talbot (1764–1800). William was a soldier and was only married four years when he died. His widow, Lady Elisabeth Fox-Strangways, had the consolation of a son, five-month-old William Henry Fox Talbot (1800–77), known as Henry. By this time the estate was deep in debt and the abbey was let until Henry came to live here with his mother and stepfather, Captain (later Admiral) Charles Feilding, in 1827. As a result of Charles's efforts, the estate was brought back out of debt and onto a more secure footing, which in part enabled Henry to pursue a life of study whilst living off a comfortable allowance.

Charles Henry Talbot succeeded his father Henry in 1877, living a quiet and scholarly life at Lacock until his death in 1916. He left the estate to his niece Matilda Gilchrist-Clark (later Talbot), who gave it to the National Trust. Her great-nephew and niece continued to live at the abbey until their deaths in 2002 and 2011.

The Abbey

Lacock Abbey is a fascinating mixture of the old, the new and the revived – medieval Gothic, Renaissance and 18th-century Gothick. With sympathy but without any attempt at symmetry, its owners have preserved layers of history that you are invited to explore.

'The remains of this grand female seclusion are more extensive, and in better preservation, than any thing of the kind within our kingdom…. Great praise is due to those who have preserved the ancient particulars … not as garden ruins, or picturesque embellishments, but as specimens of fine architecture.'

Ela, countess and abbess

'Below lie buried the bones of the venerable Ela, who gave this sacred house as a home for the nuns. She also lived here as holy abbess and countess of Salisbury, full of good works.'

This is how the Latin on Ela's tombstone in the South Cloister translates. Ela was one of the most powerful women of the Middle Ages, the only child of William, Earl of Salisbury. She was around eight when her father died and she became a ward of King Richard I. To keep her estates close at hand and give his illegitimate half-brother an income, the king married Ela to William Longespée, son of Henry II and Ida de Tosney. They had eight children and when her husband was rumoured drowned in 1225, Ela refused to consider other suitors. William had in fact been shipwrecked and returned home to Salisbury Castle only to die there the following year. He was the first person to be buried at Salisbury Cathedral having helped to lay its foundation stones with Ela in 1220.

Ela chose not to remarry and in 1227 became Sheriff of Wiltshire responsible for the rule of law as set out in the *Magna Carta*. Latin for 'great charter', this constitutional document first drawn up in 1215 and signed by King John and his barons sought to limit the powers of the king by law and protect the rights and privileges of his subjects. Ela's 1225 copy of this ground-breaking document was kept at Lacock until 1946 when it was given to the British Museum Library.

Foundress and abbess

By 1229, Ela had decided to build an abbey on her property at Lacock. The official dedication occurred on 16 April 1232 with building work continuing until at least 1247 using local limestone and 19 oaks contributed by the king. In 1240 Ela became Lacock's first abbess, serving for 17 years. She died in 1261.

Opposite The abbey from the south-east

Left The same view photographed by William Henry Fox Talbot in the mid-19th century

From abbey to country home

Although Lacock Abbey has changed a lot over its 800-year history, it remains one of Britain's most complete surviving medieval nunneries. William Sharington demolished the abbey church, but he retained most of the other buildings, leaving the cloister walks and ground-floor rooms largely intact.

On the upper floor Sharington made more drastic alterations. From 1540 he divided the large communal rooms – the nuns' dormitory, their dining room – to make smaller rooms and galleries, and he inserted a floor to create an attic level. Sharington's most impressive surviving feature is the octagonal tower added to the south-east corner on the site of the church, an important early example of French and Italian Renaissance ideas influencing English architecture. Other parts of his exterior were more predictably Tudor, like the elaborate chimneystacks of the outer courtyard that enlivened a busy roofline of gables and dormers. Sharington also added the two long stone and timber-framed ranges of stables, haylofts and grooms' quarters. The way they are layered onto the east elevation of the house gives an impression of how the rest of the exterior would have looked in his time.

Above William Sharington embellished the abbey with elaborate chimneys and decorative flourishes

THE SOUTH EAST VIEW OF LACOCK NUNNERY, IN THE COUNTY OF WIL

Nineteenth-century changes

After moving to Lacock in 1827 William Henry Fox Talbot set about modernising the abbey. The south front, which was the former internal face of the abbey church, had straight-headed windows inserted after the church was demolished. Traces of the church are still visible as arches. About 1830 Fox Talbot extended the centre part outwards and added three oriel windows in late Gothic style. The buttress to the left of these windows marks the north-west corner of the abbey church but the other buttresses date from the 1830s. Although the servants' areas were altered and new coach houses built, the abbey escaped the drastic remodelling that happened to many houses in the 19th century.

William Henry Fox Talbot's son Charles was prevented from becoming an architect by ill health but was an expert on ancient buildings. As owner of Lacock he oversaw the careful restoration of the abbey by architect Sir Harold Brakspear, as well as the repair of many village houses. He removed many of Ivory Talbot's alterations, restoring the ground floor of the east front by reinstating the missing walls and windows in 13th-century Gothic style.

Left The south-east prospect of Lacock Abbey in 1732, showing the medieval arches removed from the east front; engraving by John and Nathaniel Buck

Far left John Ivory Talbot's gothicising during the Georgian period included battlements

Top right One of the oriel windows added to the south front by William Henry Fox Talbot and the subject of the world's first photographic negative

Georgian Gothick

The abbey underwent another major change when John Ivory Talbot largely rebuilt the entrance front to create a classically proportioned Dining Room about 1752, a new hall with external stairs in the Gothick style in 1754–56, and a Gothick entrance arch in 1755. Architect Sanderson Miller was employed to revive the medieval spirit of the nunnery, although the Hall's mid-Georgian date, 1754–57, is betrayed by its symmetry and decorative detail, with central door, paired Gothick windows and two turrets with cupolas (dome-like structures). Pursuing his Romantic vision of the Middle Ages, Ivory Talbot removed Sharington's windows from the east front's arches to create an open arcade giving direct access between the surviving abbey spaces and garden. To complete the effect he added the battlements.

The Cloister

The Cloister's arcades originally ran round the entire 80-foot-square garth. In Ela's day they were simple wooden-roofed alleys with Purbeck marble columns. Sharington converted the floor above into his living quarters, with windows in striking contrast to the 15th-century arcades with their medieval Gothic traceried openings.

1 The South Cloister Walk

All the arcades of the Cloister – the South, East and North Cloister Walks (the west walk was demolished in the late 1400s) – are graced with fine stone vaulting and a fantastic range of bosses carved into heraldic shields and mythological and grotesque creatures.

Until its demolition by William Sharington, the convent church of St Mary and St Bernard stood alongside the South Cloister Walk. At the west end is a spiral stair, which gave access to the church from the abbess's lodgings above. Next to it is the **Chaplain's Room**. Women could not become priests, so the nuns had male chaplains to lead worship. The medieval plaster retains traces of wall paintings including the red outline of a late-1200s St Christopher carrying the Christ Child. Next to it is a 15th-century Crucifixion of St Andrew and on the same wall are medieval graffiti featuring hares, nuns and grotesques, signed *Johan fecit hoc* or 'John did this'.

Above The face of St Christopher on the wall painting in the Chaplain's Room

Left The exterior of the Cloister seen from the cloister court, or garth

The Sacristy was where sacred vessels and vestments were stored; the piscina next to the arched doorway was where communion vessels were washed

2 The East Cloister Walk

The well-preserved rooms along the East Cloister Walk fulfilled important functions in the daily life of the medieval abbey.

In the south corner is a single step of the night stair, which connected the church with the nuns' communal dormitory above. The **Sacristy** behind was used for storing sacred vessels and vestments. Two cupboards can still be seen on the west wall, and next to the arched doorway that once led to the church there is an original piscina, a stone basin used for washing communion vessels. The black six-pointed stars painted on the ceiling look late 1300s or early 1400s but recent analysis has concluded that they are probably 18th century. On 12 June 1754 John Ivory Talbot wrote: 'My painter (Lord Wm Seymour) is so nice and busy in Ornamenting my Cloisters.'

The nuns met daily to discuss abbey business in the **Chapter House**, so called as each day a chapter would be read from the rule that governed the abbey – the Rule of St Augustine for an Augustinian order, the Rule of St Benedict for Benedictines and Cistercians. There is evidence to suggest that Ela's original intention was to found a community of Cistercian nuns, but when the Bishop of Salisbury formally approved the foundation on 20 April 1230 he specified that the nuns should follow the Rule of St Augustine.

Although the floor was re-laid in the 19th century more than 70 different designs of tiles survive and are on show in the Servants' Hall. Featuring patterns, heraldry and animals, they were made in the mid-1200s at Naish Hill, one mile from Lacock. The Chapter House's fireplace was added by William Sharington in the 1540s.

The small space with doors to the garden is all that remains of the **Infirmary Passage**, which originally connected the abbey to its own hospital a little distance away, next to the river.

3 The Parlour and Warming House

The Parlour in the Cloister's north-east corner was the original entrance from the outer courtyard to the abbey. The stone coffins here were excavated from the **Chapter House**. After reception in the Parlour, guests would be shown to the Warming House; only this and the Chaplain's Room had a fireplace. In 1242 Henry III granted Ela one cartload of wood per week, which in 1260 she petitioned to have increased to one cartload a day. Instead Henry granted the nuns 40 acres of the Melksham Forest from which to collect wood, probably kept in the next-door storeroom. To one side of the hooded fireplace are the remains of a lamp bracket. The window seat is also original.

The large cauldron is made of bell metal inscribed with the maker's name, Peter Wagheuens of Malines (Mechelen in Belgium), and dated 1500. Originally used elsewhere in the abbey for cooking, it and its pedestal became a garden ornament in the 18th century. The stone tank was probably first used outside for washing clothes or storing fish.

Above A 15th-century mural showing a kneeling nun receiving a blessing

Left The bell metal cauldron in the Warming House

Right The North Cloister Walk

4 The North Cloister Walk

Restoration work in 1894 uncovered a richly painted mural at the end of the North Cloister Walk. Now faded, it shows a nun kneeling to receive the blessing of a bishop saint (probably Saint Augustine founder of the Augustinian Order). An inscription found in 1984 dates the mural to the time of abbess Agnes Frary (1429–45), when the rebuilding of the Cloister was completed. The nuns would have washed their hands in a large lead basin just below the painting before going upstairs to the refectory (dining room). The end bay of the walk was partitioned off before 1828 with a wall and door to create a lobby.

Service areas

The nuns' life of religious contemplation was supported by numerous servants, among them a miller, baker, brewer, swanherd, poulterer, dairymaid and cook. When the abbey became a house some rooms were adapted for service use.

1 The Servants' Hall and Wine Cellar

These rooms were once a single space below the abbey's Hall. Its fireplace, now in the Wine Cellar, dates from 1409–29. In William Sharington's time it was used for storage, subsequently becoming the beer and ale cellar. After 1827 William Henry Fox Talbot subdivided it to create these two spaces, simply furnished with tables and benches.

The central heating pipes were installed in 1876 after Amélina Petit de Billier (see page 22) set aside money in her will for the purpose. She lived at Lacock as companion to the Talbot family for more than 40 years, so must have known how welcome the extra warmth would be.

Below The Servants' Hall sparsely but practically furnished

Opposite The 'Household Wants Indicator' in the Kitchen

2 The Kitchen

Food has been cooked in this kitchen throughout the abbey's history. The fireplace, now blocked, may date from the 1300s. The window wall was moved inwards in the 1540s and another fireplace added where the cast-iron range now stands. The Gothick windows were installed by John Ivory Talbot in the 1750s. Below is an 18th-century brick stewing range with Sharington floor tiles re-used on its hobs.

Later modernisation in William Henry Fox Talbot's time included the Prize Kitchener cooking range purchased in 1845, the lead-lined wooden cabinet next to it, which is an early form of fridge, and the dumb waiter, which winched dishes upstairs to the Dining Room. The kitchen cabinet with its 'Household Wants Indicator' dates from the 1920s to the 1930s.

3 The Cooking Room

From 1929 Matilda Talbot gave cookery demonstrations in this room using the Valour Paraffin Cooker with its handy extra hot plates under a removable top oven. Women from upper-class backgrounds were beginning to take jobs in the early 20th century. Matilda was a trained cook and passed on her knowledge teaching in a number of London schools. She also volunteered in a French Red Cross canteen during the First World War (1914–18). She promoted good food at Lacock, hosting an exhibition to showcase Britain's regional dishes in the abbey's Hall. During the food shortages of the Second World War (1939–45), she showed local people how to make the most of their rations.

'My niece is a Greenwich cook, who has been presented at Court.'

Rosamond Talbot

Uncovering an amazing collection

Only Lacock's portraits were included in the 1944 gift to the National Trust. The rest of the collection was purchased from the donor family in 2009. Display cases in the Servants' Hall show some of its medieval treasures: original encaustic tiles and the only manuscript from an English abbey to have survived in the building where it was created. *Expositiones Vocabulorum Bibliae* is a reference book used by the nuns, a dictionary of difficult words used in the Bible. (Its shorter title is the Brito as it was compiled by William Brito.) It has been at Lacock for more than 700 years.

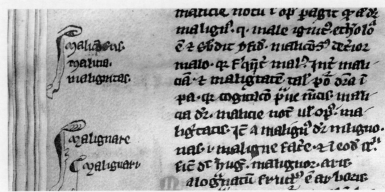

The Brown Gallery

When William Sharington converted the abbey into a country house he partitioned the nuns' refectory to make the Brown Gallery and the numerous rooms off it. He inserted a ceiling into the open roof space but two medieval corbels (brackets) can still be seen, one made of wood, the other a carved stone head.

Family portraits hanging here include Matilda Talbot, painted in 1949 by Lord Methuen RA, her friend and neighbour at Corsham Court (see page 5). The war artist John Piper's striking *View of Lacock Abbey* was painted after he stayed here in 1942. In a cabinet are geological specimens believed to have been collected by William Henry Fox Talbot and his son Charles.

Below *View of Lacock Abbey*, by John Piper, 1942

Food for body and soul

The nuns sat at long tables in their refectory, overlooked by the abbess on a raised dais. They often ate mutton from sheep bred on abbey lands or fish from their own stewponds and the River Avon. Only one nun was allowed to break the silence of mealtimes. Standing in a pulpit (in what is now the Pulpit Room) she would read to her sisters.

The Brown Gallery was created when William Sharington partitioned the nuns' dining room

The Pulpit Room and Yellow Room

Most of Lacock's family rooms, including bedrooms, are on the upper floor. In the 19th century William Henry Fox Talbot updated these bedrooms with late Gothic-style fireplaces. His granddaughter Matilda made further alterations to create the bathroom, with its touch of interwar Art Deco on the panelled bath.

Matilda slept in the Pulpit Room, which, with the help of her niece, Janet Burnett-Brown, has been arranged to evoke her era. Among the possessions on display is a dressing table tray that belonged to Matilda and was presented to her in 1919 by the Women's Royal Naval Service (WRNS), with whom she served during the First World War.

Below The Pulpit Room

Matilda Talbot (1871–1958)

Matilda Gilchrist-Clark was born in Scotland where her father ran the Duke of Buccleuch's Drumlanrig estate in Dumfries. As the fifth of six children she never dreamt that her grandfather's abbey would one day be hers. An independent-minded woman with a talent for languages, she was also an intrepid traveller making her first foreign trip to the Faroe Islands aged 22. On her return she began training to be a cookery teacher, lodging in London with her favourite aunt, Rosamond. When Rosamond returned to Lacock to look after her bachelor brother Charles Talbot, Matilda went with her. She stayed after her aunt's death in 1906 but was still surprised when she, rather than her brother, inherited Lacock on her uncle's death in 1916. She changed her name to Talbot in 1918. In 1932 she led a pageant dressed as Ela, celebrating Lacock's 700th anniversary. Matilda never married and devoted herself to caring for Lacock and her tenants. In 1944 she secured the future of her ancestral home by giving it to the National Trust.

The Stone Gallery

This room was originally part of the nuns' dormitory. William Sharington inserted the ceiling and created a Long Gallery on the floor above that led out onto the rooftops and to his banqueting chamber at the top of the tower. His Renaissance-style carved stone fireplace was probably the creation of master mason John Chapman.

A facsimile of Sharington's portrait drawn by Hans Holbein (see page 25) is displayed in a case next to examples of the encaustic tiles he used to decorate his floors. Some are personalised with a scorpion, his heraldic symbol. The huge pestle and mortar made of bell metal also bears a Sharington scorpion. It dates from the 1540s and was listed among kitchen utensils in a 1575 inventory.

The Gothick Talbots

In the mid-18th century John Ivory Talbot 'gothicised' Sharington's windows with arched lights incorporating medieval glass fragments. His portrait hangs on the west wall with that of his wife Mary Mansel, both painted by Michael Dahl (1656–1743). Other portraits include Ivory Talbot's mother Anne Talbot, and his sister Barbara Davenport, owner of the large early 18th-century leather-covered chest.

Below John Ivory Talbot's wife, Mary Mansel, painted by Michael Dahl

Right One of Lacock's rare 17th-century *sgabello* chairs, a piece of furniture typical of the Italian Renaissance period

Far right A watercolour of the Stone Gallery painted in 1914 by Matilda Gilchrist-Clark (Matilda Talbot after 1918)

Left A medieval stained glass panel in the Stone Gallery, part of John Ivory Talbot's gothicising of the abbey

Shells and horns

The six shell-backed chairs are of a rare Italian form known as *sgabello*, probably made in London around 1635. The Talbots' heraldic lion was painted in later. Above the fireplace is a large set of moose antlers, probably brought back from Canada by William Davenport Talbot, who served as a soldier there in 1791–92.

The practicalities of prayer

Ela's nuns slept on beds with straw mattresses separated by screens in a large room open to the roof. At three o'clock in the morning they began matins, the first of their eight daily prayers, descending straight to the church via the night stair. They wore white woollen tunics topped with a mantle that was lined with white cloth in summer and fur in winter. This habit was completed by a fur pilch (cloak), a veil and a wimple.

The Tapestry Room
The Cloister Room

Toys of the Talbots
In the little dressing room is a display of toys enjoyed by children from the abbey's past. Matilda Talbot fondly recalled the rocking horse bought by her grandfather William Henry Fox Talbot in about 1840: 'He was called Firefoot because we said he galloped so fast that he struck fire from the stones in the road.'

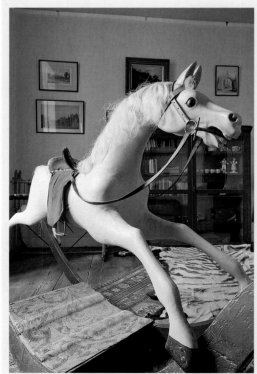

1 The Tapestry Room
Also once part of the nuns' dormitory, the Tapestry Room got its name from a set of fine 17th-century tapestries woven at the Mortlake factory near London; they were sold in 1918 to fund building repairs in the village. The mahogany four-poster bed, with original chintz (glazed printed cotton) hangings, was made around 1825.

2 The Cloister Room
This room overlooks the Cloister and would have had lancet windows when it was part of the medieval dormitory. (A lancet window is a tall, narrow window with a pointed arch at its top, so-called for its resemblance to a lance.) The patterned wallpaper was made in 1810 by Williams, Cooper & Boyle, a firm active in Southfield, London.

Above The Tapestry Room and the Tapestry Dressing Room beyond

Right Early 19th-century wallpaper by Williams, Cooper & Boyle in the Cloister Room

The Short Lobby

The early Victorian bookcases and their fragile contents were moved here from the Blue Parlour by Matilda Talbot. In the far right-hand corner of the room is an elegant panelled door, which once led to the staircase to the Long Gallery. Today it simply conceals a cupboard.

Below This small room was once part of the nuns' dormitory

The Ante Room and Upper East Room

Leading one into the other, these rooms were part of a Sharington extension on the outer wall of the nuns' dormitory.

The Ante Room and Upper East Room have wallpapers with Chinese-inspired designs made in the 1830s, chosen by William Henry Fox Talbot's family. The paper in the Ante Room was made by Duppa, Slodden & Collins of Oxford Street, London. In places an earlier 19th-century paper with a design of jasmine plants can also be seen. The Upper East Room wallpaper is embossed to give a realistic imitation of watered silk, very fashionable at the time. It may be the only one of its kind that survives *in situ*.

Amélina Petit de Billier

Born in Paris in 1798, Amélina died at Lacock in 1876 and was buried in the Talbot family grave. She was governess to Caroline and Horatia Feilding and spent the majority of her life as a trusted companion living and travelling with their parents Lady Elisabeth and Captain Charles Feilding, before becoming a permanent fixture in the household of Lady Elisabeth's son, William Henry Fox Talbot. Fifteen of her journals survive from 1820–35 describing, in her native French, the titled and famous people she met, the foreign countries she visited and family life at Lacock. Her wooden writing box (pictured) is in the Upper East Room where she slept. Surviving letters to William Henry Fox Talbot show her fascination for his endeavours in photography and a shared interest in botany. She was also a keen musician, able to sing as well as play the harp and piano.

Above **The Upper East Room with its embossed imitation silk wallpaper**

Opposite (clockwise from top left)
St Michael's Mount by Matilda Gilchrist-Clark (Talbot after 1918)

Hall at Cothele by Matilda Glichrist-Clark (Talbot after 1918)

Castel Nuova, Naples by Rosamond Talbot

The Painting Room

This room was used as a studio by William Henry Fox Talbot's three daughters Ela, Rosamond and Matilda. Paintings by various members of the Talbot family now hang on the walls.

The Tower Room

The Tower Room, a heavily protected strong room for the display of Sharington's most precious objects, is perhaps unique in England. It may have precedents in the lost royal strong rooms of Whitehall and Greenwich Palaces. Sharington was Groom of the Chamber to Henry VIII and would have known about the storage of royal treasures.

For all its security features, this room was also about showing off. Emblazoned with the Sharington scorpion, it was a place where Sharington could display his treasures on the central table to favoured guests. For centuries the Lacock papers, including the Lacock copy of the 1225 *Magna Carta*, were kept here. On the floor above Sharington created a fashionable rooftop banqueting room (not accessible), where in the 1500s small groups would go after a meal, to be served sweet delicacies and admire the view. Another example from the 1560s is at Longleat, owned by Sharington's friend Sir John Thynne.

Left The stone table in the Tower Room supported by grinning satyrs

Opposite The stone boss on the ceiling, carved with the scorpion emblem and initials of Sir William Sharington

A man of sophistication

This extremely rare stone table bears the ciphers of William Sharington and his third wife Grace, whom he married in 1542. There is another in the banqueting room on the floor above. Both show Sharington's sophisticated tastes, with designs inspired by cutting edge Flemish and Italian design. The octagonal top is supported by grinning satyrs carrying bursting buckets of ripe fruit. The superb carving is attributed to John Chapman, who also worked for Henry VIII, John Dudley, and Sir John Thynne at Longleat, members of an elite group experimenting with Continental ideas. Sharington had been to France on a diplomatic mission with Thomas Seymour, and later shared his architectural knowledge with John Dudley, at whose Dudley Castle there is a wing named after him. These were the men who got him respectively into and out of trouble (see box). The Tudor court was made up of closely guarded and fiercely competing cliques and alliances, and there are clear indications, even statements, in his conversion of Lacock Abbey that Sharington shared not only his friends' political allegiances but also their architectural tastes.

Sir William Sharington (c.1495–1553)

William Sharington came from a minor Norfolk gentry family but made good connections, rising to power as a protégé of Sir Thomas Seymour, brother of Henry VIII's third queen, Jane Seymour. He was appointed Page of the King's Robes and this chalk drawing of him by Hans Holbein the Younger is in the Royal Collection at Windsor Castle. He reaped rich rewards by acquiring land and property from the religious houses closed down in the Dissolution of the Monasteries in the 1530s. He purchased Lacock in 1540 for £783, and bought monastic lands across southern England including nearby Avebury. He traded in wool, lent money and had several merchant ships at Bristol, including the *Scorpion*. (His heraldic symbol, the scorpion, can be seen throughout Lacock and suggests a man you had to watch quite carefully.) In 1546 he was appointed under-treasurer of the new Bristol mint, where he enriched himself even further by illegally clipping the coins it issued. The following year Sir Thomas Seymour's nine-year-old nephew was crowned King Edward VI. Sharington's connections saw him rewarded with a knighthood. With a young, impressionable king on the throne, court factions were jockeying for influence, and Sharington became involved in a plot led by Sir Thomas against Seymour's brother Edward, Duke of Somerset, the king's uncle and protector. The plot was discovered and both Sir Thomas and Sharington were arrested. Sharington was charged with various frauds and 'clapt up' in the Tower of London on 19 January 1549, his lands confiscated. He confessed, implicating his former friend and ally Sir Thomas, who was executed for treason. Eight months later, when another influential friend John Dudley, Duke of Northumberland, took over government, Sharington was pardoned, released and allowed to buy back his property for £12,867 (some £6 million today). In 1550 he was appointed a commissioner for the sale of Boulogne – then English property – to the King of France, and two years later, a year before he died, had restored his reputation sufficiently to be appointed Sheriff of Wiltshire.

The Blue Parlour

This room was William Henry Fox Talbot's library. After inheriting in 1916, his granddaughter Matilda removed the bookcases to reveal panelling dating from around 1700–20, contemporary with the fireplace and sash windows. She records in her autobiography that by happy coincidence her choice of light blue walls was almost identical to the colour shown in an 1829 watercolour of the room.

The portrait of a man in a blue coat to the right of the door is Sanderson Miller, the architect of the abbey's Gothick Hall, painted about 1750 (see page 33). To the left of the fireplace is a portrait of John Talbot, son of John Ivory Talbot, painted by Thomas Gainsborough in the 1760s.

An even more famous name is linked to the desk, made about 1825 and called a Carlton House desk, after the London home of the Prince Regent, later George IV, for whom the design was supposedly first made. It is believed to have been given by Queen Victoria in payment for a gambling debt incurred by her father, the Duke of Kent.

The fragile 19th-century carpet was woven in Aubusson, central France and came here from Markeaton Hall, the Derbyshire home (now demolished) of Fox Talbot's wife, Constance Mundy.

Below left The Blue Parlour

Below Portrait of John Talbot, by Thomas Gainsborough

A splendid library

In 2009 the National Trust acquired Lacock's collection of almost 4,000 books, spanning the late 13th to the 20th centuries. Few houses have a library with so many layers of history, and which so obviously reflects the interests of its occupants over many centuries. The pictured book plates represent a very small sample of the subjects of interest to Lacock's owners and cover: geography (*A New Sett of Maps both of Antient and Present*, 1706); history (*Historiae Danicae Libri XVI* ['Sixteen Books on Danish History'], published 1644; and botany (a 1552 edition by Hieronymus Bock, *De Stirpium* ['On Plants']). Research into the volumes now spread throughout the abbey has revealed an exceptionally early numbering and cataloguing system from the 1600s, when someone at the abbey was using the new method of shelving their books with spines facing out rather than in.

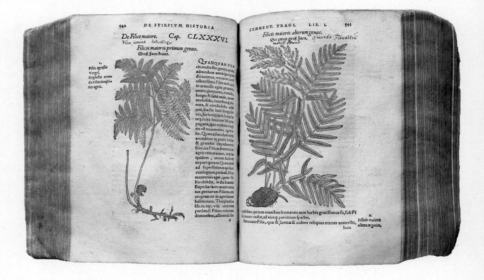

The South Gallery

From the late 1300s this gallery was a corridor between the nuns' dormitory and the abbess's chapel, a separate space at the refectory end, all built over the South Cloister Walk. Sharington increased its height and created an elaborately patterned tiled floor with his scorpion badge.

When William Henry Fox Talbot moved to Lacock in 1827 he set about making it into the pleasant family sitting room described by governess Amélina in her journal, enlarging it with three oriel windows. In an age when music was the most popular form of evening entertainment, the family, Amélina and guests, notably the famous Irish poet and songwriter Thomas Moore who lived near Lacock, often filled the gallery with songs, piano playing and the beautiful sound of the 'Angel' harp made by Sébastien Erard.

The stone fireplaces and door-cases inserted by William Henry Fox Talbot are in late Gothic style, their details echoed in the mouldings and shafts of the bookcases and ceiling.

Far left The South Gallery

Left The 'Angel' harp being played by William Henry Fox Talbot's half-sister Horatia Feilding

Opposite The history-making South Gallery oriel window

A window into photographic history

Possibly the most important artefact in photographic history is a tiny negative made in this room by William Henry Fox Talbot. In August 1835 he captured an image of the central oriel window in which the light and dark tones were reversed. It was so perfect that all 200 diamond-shaped panes of glass could be counted with a magnifying glass. A copy of the original negative hangs next to the window.

Latticed Window
(with the Camera Obscura)
August 1835
When first made, the squares
of glass about 200 in number
could be counted, with help
of a lens.

'... three large Gothic windows had been added to the South Gallery. One of these bay windows is so large that it makes a kind of drawing room where there are tables, sofas, etc. ... in each is a writing table … it makes a very large, comfortable and artistic room.'

Amélina Petit de Billier's journal,
11 September 1831

The Dining Room

In March 1752 John Ivory Talbot was billed for 'pediments and other architectural details' to ornament his newly built Dining Room. The restrained Classical style he chose here is markedly different from his dramatically Gothick Hall, which was constructed soon after.

The door-cases with curved brackets supporting triangular pediments, the fireplace, the built-in moulded picture frames and the frieze between walls and ceiling are characteristic of the Palladian style which developed in England from about 1715 onwards. It was inspired by the work of Italian architect Andrea Palladio (1508–80), which in turn derived from ancient Greek and Roman temple architecture.

The elaborately carved pier-table and mirror in the much more decorative Rococo style were supplied in 1750 by Henry Hill, a cabinet-maker from Marlborough. Hill also carved the fireplace and frieze. The four glass lanterns, each designed to hold a single candle, were moved here from the Hall.

Family meals were always eaten in the Dining Room until Matilda Talbot was inspired by the original oak floor to turn it into a ballroom. As she recalled in her memoirs, 'We held a dance in it soon after the end of the first war, and since then we have danced in it more times than I can count.'

John Ivory Talbot (?1691–1772)
In an octagonal frame above the door to the Hall is a copy of Michael Dahl's portrait of John Ivory Talbot, the man behind the Georgian transformation of Lacock. This portrait was cut out of a larger painting and inserted into the frame. The painting with its octagonal hole, still in its frame, remains in the collection. The eldest grandson of Sir John Talbot and his wife Barbara Slingsby, John Ivory inherited the estate in 1714 joining the Talbot name to his own. He was married to the heiress Mary Mansel, whose property of Margam in Glamorgan descended to their second son, Thomas Talbot. Thomas's grandson developed Port Talbot, as a result of which he was said to be the richest commoner in England. He was a genial and hospitable host, described by his architect Sanderson Miller as a 'very agreeable companion'. His alterations to the house sought to remove Tudor work and, with the notable exception of the Dining Room, restore a feeling of the medieval past as interpreted through the 18th-century Gothick style. In the garden he employed well-known designers to create water features and new park landscapes.

Strongly Classical details in the Dining Room and *Peace and the Arts*, by Cornelis van Haarlem over the fireplace

The art of shell collecting

The painting above the fireplace is a mid-18th century copy of an early 17th-century Dutch portrait of shell collector Jan Govertsen van der Aer (*c.*1544–1612). Dressed in blue and holding one of his shells, he is surrounded by allegorical figures representing music, painting and sculpture. The naked figure on the left holds the olive branch of peace and the horn of plenty (cornucopia). The weapons of war lie abandoned at her feet.

The Hall

Sanderson Miller (1716–80)

William Pitt hailed Miller as the 'Great Master of Gothic' but his architectural work was always an amateur interest, secondary to the running of his estate at Radway in Warwickshire. A childhood interest in medieval history led Miller to gothicise buildings on his own land, beginning with a gate lodge designed as a sham castle overlooking the Civil War battlefield at Edgehill. His talent for designing ready-made ruins found a receptive audience among friends who wanted their own garden follies. Miller's coat of arms appears on the north wall of Lacock's Hall and his portrait now hangs in the Blue Parlour, an unusual honour for an architect.

John Ivory Talbot dismissed Lacock's Tudor hall as 'Horrid!' and rebuilt it from 1754–56. He kept the medieval undercroft (now the Servants' Hall and Wine Cellar) because 'my Regard to ye Antiquity of it, is such, that I cannot Prevail with myself to give it any disturbance'.

No local architect working in the Gothick style could be found so a friend recommended Sanderson Miller, who persuaded his client to have a flat pair of windows either side of the door instead of the bow windows he had intended. These windows feature stained glass from the nunnery salvaged by Ivory Talbot. Miller designed the Gothick cornice and canopied wall niches, as well as the door-cases and chimneypiece, which were carved by Robert Parsons of Bath. In tribute to Ela, the chimneypiece features an abbess's mitre.

The barrel-vaulted ceiling is painted with 45 heraldic shields. Ivory Talbot planned to mark its completion with a party 'when all my friends who are in the country and whose arms are emblazoned on the ceiling will do me the honour of their company and a grand sacrifice to Bacchus (the Roman god of wine and revelry) will be the consequence'.

The brass andirons in the fireplace were installed by Sanderson Miller, who described them as 'antique' having been made about 1680. The yew-wood tables were probably commissioned for this room and the chairs are of about the same date.

Fired figures

The Hall's terracotta sculptures were made on site in 1755–56 by Austrian modeller Victor Alexander Sederbach. They were mostly fired in a large kiln in the orchard and took eight months to complete. In January 1756 John Ivory Talbot wrote to Sanderson Miller: 'I presume you are acquainted with the method of making Models for Statues. He proceeds on the same Principles, only Bakes them afterwards, by which means they become of a Red Colour and ring like a Garden Pot.' Ela takes pride of place above the chimneypiece flanked by two granddaughters who entered the abbey as nuns. Her husband, William Longespée, is probably the man wearing an earl's coronet holding a church plan above the door in the far wall. Facing him is his father King Henry II. The knight in armour is Ela's eldest son, another William, who died in Egypt whilst on Crusade. Her youngest son Nicholas, Bishop of Salisbury, is shown in his mitre. Of the other symbolic representations, the winged and crowned skeleton of death is the most striking.

Opposite The Hall, c.1830/40, by Nicholas Condy (1793–1857)

Right The sugar lump was first placed on the goat's nose by a student in 1919

The Stable Court

William Sharington built the ranges that enclose this courtyard in the 1540s, reputedly using stone from the demolished abbey church. Any irregularities would have been covered up by lime render, which survives in white patches. John Ivory Talbot formed the gateway in the 1750s; the earlier entrance was through a two-storey medieval gatehouse on the other side of the Gothick arch – a blocked arch survives.

Sharington's buildings contain stables, a brewhouse and other working spaces. Despite their more humble functions, these were meant to be seen. The doorways and mouldings are of a sophisticated design and the scrolled brackets to the dormer windows are a particular Sharington trademark.

The irregular southern side of the court with an arched first-floor window contains the former nuns' refectory range with roof built in the 1400s. The lower ground level is the site of a medieval range demolished in about 1828. Near the far corner of the court a single column attached to the wall and a blocked upper doorway, dating from Sharington's time, may be the remains of a first-floor gallery.

An inventory taken in 1778 records the stable yard full of agricultural and garden paraphernalia including '1 Plow, 3 Harrows' and '4 Wheelbarrows'. In the stables were four carthorses and one horse for pulling a hackney carriage. In the late 1700s, in addition to stabling and a brewhouse, there was a fruit room, harness room, dairy, washhouse, laundry and a granary. At this date the abbey also had its own engine house for 'a fire Engine and pipes compleat'. The low range of coach houses was added by William Henry Fox Talbot around 1838.

Below The clock-tower in the Tudor Stable Court is framed in the Gothick arch commissioned by John Ivory Talbot

Below left The Stable Court, photographed by William Henry Fox Talbot in the mid-19th century

The Brewhouse and Bakehouse

The abbey has always had a brewhouse because weak beer, made from barley, was the main drink for most people including servants, until well into the 1800s. Until then most country houses had a brewhouse. The usual allowance was a gallon of ale a day, which would have been made on site.

Sharington's Brewhouse occupies two rooms to the right of the clock-tower. Its continued use over some 200 years required the replacement of original brewing equipment but the Brewhouse remains a well-preserved and rare example of its type. Most of the brewing process happened in the larger room but the small room contains the fireplace that heated the copper boiler, which is set in a raised stone surround next door.

How to brew
The brew started with water, which was run off into the mash tun below the copper once it had reached a rolling boil. Malt was then added and the mixture stirred for two hours. It went back into the copper, the hops were added and the mix reheated. The liquid was then run off into the large wooden cooling tray to drain into the shallow barrel, called a fermenting tun, underneath. With the addition of yeast it was left to ferment for two to seven days.

Mythical beasts
Getting up close to gargoyles is rarely possible but on the wall of the Bakehouse there are stone replicas of the fantastical creatures guarding Sharington's country house. Detailed copies have been made of these original features in anticipation of the day when the effects of atmospheric erosion make replacement necessary.

Above The Brewhouse

Below A replica of the Tudor carved stone gargoyles on the Bakehouse wall

The Garden

There are many layers of history in the abbey gardens. Going back to the 13th century, they kept the community of nuns supplied with vegetables, fruit, medicinal herbs, and even fish from the stewponds. Evolved over centuries into fashionable and pleasing grounds, they also nourish the senses.

After Lacock became a private residence in 1540 William Sharington introduced a more ornamental layout. No details survive but the homes of other Tudor courtiers boasted very formal knot gardens and parterres of highly complex designs. The earliest surviving estate plan dates from 1714 when the grounds to the south and west of the abbey included the Lady's Garden, the Fountain Garden and the Lower Garden.

Wonderful water gardens

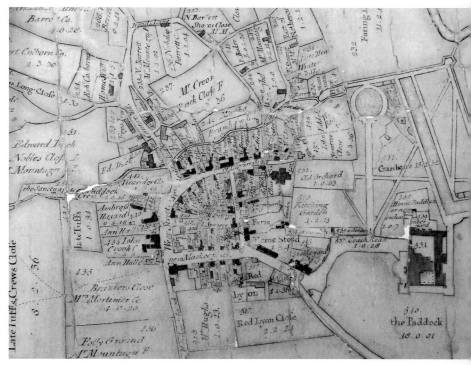

Soon after inheriting Lacock in 1714, John Ivory Talbot began updating the gardens with fashionable long canals, some based on the medieval stewponds. From 1722 he was advised by landscape designer Stephen Switzer, who also worked at Blenheim and Castle Howard. Little survives of this scheme except for the pair of Tuscan columns topped with an 18th-century sphinx on the old *patte d'oie* (a point from which straight walks radiate, from the French 'foot of the goose'). This once marked the head of a tree-lined walk north towards a large circular pool called the 'Great Bason'. Other straight paths criss-crossed the garden towards an L-shaped canal, creating sight lines into the wider landscape. Additional Georgian features included an obelisk and what Ivory Talbot called his 'rockworks', a surviving arched grotto over the Bide Brook begun in 1749. The rockworks still ornament the garden but the obelisk has since vanished.

With these new water works the garden's focus shifted north of the house. By 1764 the old formal gardens to the south had been replaced with a terrace overlooking a new area of parkland, separated from it by a ha-ha (a turfed ditch designed to keep grazing livestock out of the garden without obstructing the view). Ivory Talbot wrote to Sanderson Miller about having made 'an handsome Sweep for a Coach and Six and built the Ah Ah likewise in front of the Hall'.

The present abbey drive was laid out about 1754 to maximise the impact of Ivory Talbot's Gothick improvements. Tantalising visitors with a glimpse of the abbey, it disappears into woodland re-emerging to a view of the entrance front framed by Miller's Gothick arch. Miller's friend, Lancelot Capability Brown, was employed at Lacock during the 1750s but his exact contribution is unclear.

From 1780 landscape designer William Emes altered the formal geometric gardens to create a more naturalistic design with sinuous lines. As well as shortening the canal he added a two-part serpentine lake and a round pond with an island. These were all filled in during the 1840s.

'I am about so handsome a work, that … when finished will be as surprising & agreeable as any gardens in England.'

John Ivory Talbot to Henry Davenport, 7 November 1719

Above A map of the estate from 1764 showing the Kitchen Garden as well as ornamental features such as the 'Great Bason'

Opposite A foggy day in autumn in the grounds at Lacock Abbey

Lady Elisabeth's Rose Garden

Dismantled in the 1960s, Lady Elisabeth's Rose Garden was reinstated in 1991 using the original arches, which had been stored above the Brewhouse.

William Henry Fox Talbot's mother, Lady Elisabeth Fox-Strangways, was a dominant influence upon his garden as well as his life. She had never lived at Lacock with Henry's father as the abbey was tenanted at that time, so when she arrived in 1827 it was with her second husband Captain (later Admiral) Charles Feilding and their daughters Caroline and Horatia. She laid out her rose garden soon after, centred on an urn surrounded by trellised iron arches.

Henry's sisters, wife and daughters also tended their own garden plots, often writing about them in their letters. After Caroline married Ernest, 3rd Earl of Mount Edgcumbe, plants were frequently swapped between their homes at Mount Edgcumbe, Cotehele and Lacock.

The Botanic and Kitchen Gardens

The Botanic Garden

William Henry Fox Talbot showed an interest in botany as a young boy, and when he was only 29 he was elected a fellow of the prestigious Linnean Society dedicated to the study of natural history. In 1838 he used his influence there, as well as considerable family and political connections, to help his friend Sir William Jackson Hooker save Kew Gardens for the nation.

In his own botanic garden at Lacock, within the 18th-century walls of a former stable yard, Fox Talbot built lean-to greenhouses and a conservatory where he could grow and propagate tender plants. He was especially interested in phenology – the seasonal timing of flowering or seeding – and his desire to record plant material undoubtedly influenced his experiments with photography. He brought plants back from his travels, collected euphorbias and orchids, and introduced rare specimen trees.

The Kitchen Garden

Food has always been grown in the garden at the abbey. It supplied the nuns, and then the Sharington and Talbot families. In the early 1700s a walled kitchen garden was created. Its layout was altered around 1754, and during Henry's day at least both it and the Botanic Garden flourished. When the Talbots were away from Lacock, hampers of garden produce would be sent to them in London or Edinburgh.

Charles Talbot did not share his father's passion for plants. Charles's niece Matilda was left with very little money to pay staff and the gardens declined. By the time Lacock passed to the National Trust in 1944 the Botanic Garden had been turned into allotments for the village. The Kitchen Garden is still used by villagers.

Opposite Lady Elisabeth's Rose Garden photographed in 1841 by William Henry Fox Talbot

Far left The greenhouse in the Botanic Garden

Left *Echinacea purpurea* (cone flower)

Above Blue *Eryngium bourgatii* and *Allium christophii* in the Botanic Garden

The garden today

William Henry Fox Talbot was the last owner to make major changes to the grounds so the re-opening of his Botanic Garden in 1999 was an important step towards revealing Lacock's many hidden layers.

A late-Victorian estate map provided the position of paths and borders. The glasshouses against the wall were reinstated on their old foundations in 2004–08. The plants inside have been chosen to reflect the types of fruit, vegetables and flowers grown here by the Talbot family. In the wider garden the aim is to draw out historic elements that enhance Lacock's spirit of place as somewhere that is peaceful, tranquil and timeless.

A view into the evening sun
in September in the garden
at Lacock Abbey

The Fox Talbot Museum

Lacock's most famous owner made many contributions to scholarship but the museum in his honour celebrates his world-changing breakthroughs in photography.

The Fox Talbot Museum opened in 1975 in a 16th-century barn once used as stables. It houses a collection spanning the history of photography up to the present day, with a mezzanine gallery for temporary exhibitions. One of the museum's main aims is to give local and international visitors the opportunity, through workshops and demonstrations, to explore historic photographic processes, and in particular the techniques of William Henry Fox Talbot and his rival, French inventor Louis Daguerre.

William Henry Fox Talbot

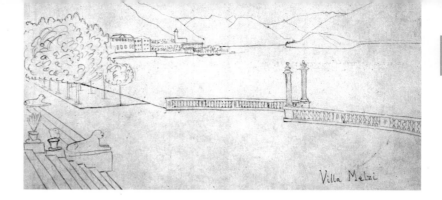

William Henry Fox Talbot was five months old when he inherited Lacock. His father had left him an estate £30,000 in debt but his mother's remarriage in 1804 to Captain Charles Feilding provided a sympathetic stepfather whose careful management secured Lacock's future and allowed the young boy to concentrate on his studies.

William Henry Fox Talbot (or Henry as the family called him and as we shall call him in this chapter) was a keen student. At Harrow he spent his pocket money on chemistry equipment and compiled an index of local flora. He left top of his class going on to study mathematics at Trinity College, Cambridge, where he also won the Porson Prize for Greek verse. In the wake of the 18th-century Enlightenment, there was no limit to what a curious mind with a university education might achieve, and Henry's curiosity was wide-ranging.

Foreign travels

After leaving Harrow, Henry made his first visit to Europe with his stepfather. Although he could legally take possession of Lacock in 1821, the abbey was let to a local MP, so Henry and his family chose to live abroad until the house became vacant six years later. In 1824 he met fellow scientist John Herschel in Munich. Their friendship was also an important scientific collaboration and the influence of Herschel as well as Sir David Brewster (whom he met through Herschel in 1826) probably led Henry towards research on light and optics.

At the end of 1832 Henry married Constance Mundy of Markeaton Hall in Derbyshire. Almost simultaneously he was elected to parliament as a Whig candidate intent on political reform. This meant waiting for their honeymoon until June 1833. The only way to record the places they saw during their six-month European honeymoon was with pen and brush, but drawing was not one of Henry's gifts. Particularly frustrated by his efforts to capture the scenery of Lake Como in northern Italy, he pondered whether science could provide a solution.

Opposite **William Henry Fox Talbot photographed by John Moffat of Edinburgh in 1866**

Above **Sketch of the Villa Metzi made by William Henry Fox Talbot using a camera obscura during his honeymoon in Italy**

Left **Constance Talbot, née Mundy; the couple married in 1832**

Experiments and discoveries

'How charming it would be if it were possible to cause these natural images to imprint themselves durably, and remain fixed on paper.'

William Henry Fox Talbot,
5 October 1833

Henry could not get on with the drawing aids of the time because the scenes their lenses projected onto paper still had to be sketched out by hand. The camera lucida (in Latin, 'light room') was a small prism on top of a brass stem, while the portable camera obscura ('dark room) was a box in which views were reflected onto ground glass for the artist to trace. Henry understood that at its most basic, the picture was simply a succession of lights and shadows thrown onto different parts of the paper. He began experimenting with ways to permanently capture these using chemistry on his return to Lacock in spring 1834.

Shadow drawings

Henry started by coating sheets of ordinary writing paper with alternate washes of table salt and silver nitrate. He placed an opaque object like a leaf, onto this light-sensitive paper and left it in the sun. The uncovered areas darkened leaving a silhouette where the leaf had been. He called these contact prints sciagraphs (Greek for 'shadow drawings'). The next challenge was to stabilise the images and by autumn 1834 Henry had found that a wash of potassium iodide could be used to fix them.

Left Two of Henry's 'mousetrap' cameras, c. 1835

Above and right Henry's early experiments with sodium chloride and silver nitrate yielded encouraging results: from left to right 'Fern Leaf', 1836…

…and 'Bryonia dioica – The English Wild Vine', c.1839…

…'Astrantia major – The Melancholy Gentleman', 1838

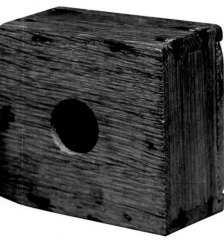

The summer of '35

The long, hot summer of 1835 encouraged Henry to increase the sensitivity of his coated paper and attempt pictures of buildings using a modified camera obscura. Little wooden boxes made by the Lacock carpenter were fitted with microscope lenses and left around the abbey grounds to gather light. Constance nicknamed them 'mousetraps' and Henry himself described their tiny pictures as the work of 'Lilliputian artists'. His first successful in-camera image was of the central oriel window in Lacock's South Gallery (see page 29).

Importantly for the future of photography, Henry also grasped that a single 'negative' could produce multiple 'positive' copies (terms coined by Sir John Herschel). The light values could be returned to their original state by exposing a new sheet of light-sensitive paper through the negative.

The rush to be first

At the beginning of 1839 an announcement came from Paris that Louis Daguerre had frozen the images from a camera obscura. Henry had been busy with other things over the intervening years and it now looked like he had missed a crucial opportunity and he was too late in going public with his findings. Daguerre was hailed as the 'father of photography' and lavishly rewarded by the French government. Without a repeat of that summer of 1835 and without support from the British establishment, 1839 was a very gloomy year for Henry.

The calotype

The sunshine returned in early 1840 and so did Henry's enthusiasm for developing his process. He made a brilliant observation that significantly reduced exposure times when he discovered that an image was captured by his silver paper within seconds of its exposure to sunlight. By using gallic acid as a chemical developer this latent image could be made into a full-strength negative and by the same means faded negatives could be revived. His mother urged him to call the technique the Talbotype but when the public announcement was made in spring 1841 Henry chose calotype, from the Greek *kalos* meaning 'beautiful'.

Patent problems

After losing out to Daguerre the previous year Henry was understandably wary about declaring his improved process to the world. He decided to take out a patent. Far from solving his problems this actually increased them. Anyone wanting to use the calotype commercially needed to apply to him for a licence but Henry was not a businessman and handled the necessary administration poorly. Once he had licensees, however, Henry felt duty-bound to protect the rights they had bought even though it provoked fierce criticism that his money-grabbing was hindering the development of photography. This was not at all fair. Henry never made any money from licensing and his patent did not restrict scientific use of the calotype, yet such accusations did long-lasting damage to his reputation.

Above **The Reading Establishment**, *c.*1846, including an engraving being photographed (left), a camera being operated (centre), printing frames holding negatives and paper being 'printed out' by sunlight (centre right), Nicholas Henneman photographing a sculpture of 'The Three Graces' (right) and a device, thought to be a focimeter, to assist in focusing (far right)

Left *The Pencil of Nature*, Issue No.1, 1844–46

The Daguerrotype had so quickly become established as the primary photographic process – indeed Henry's self-portraits used his competitor's method – that Henry was finding it difficult to attract interest in his new technique. To try to remedy the apparent lack of interest in his calotype Henry began publication of *The Pencil of Nature* in June 1844. The world's first-ever photographic book, it was designed to map out photography's future uses in portraiture, architecture, landscape, still-life and documentation. Subscribers were issued with six parts before the project was abandoned in April 1846.

The book's 24 prints are among the most beautiful images of early photography. They were made by Dutchman Nicholas Henneman, Henry's former valet and later photographic assistant, who ran the Reading Establishment, Henry's printing studio, half-way between Lacock and London. He printed Henry's *Sunpictures* in Scotland featuring views of places in Sir Walter Scott's poetry in 1845, and 7,000 prints to accompany the June 1846 issue of the *Art-Union Journal*. Henneman also offered his services to other photographers who wanted their negatives printed by a professional. Although not a commercial success, the pioneering establishment produced more than 50,000 prints using sunlight in the three years before its closure in 1847.

Life at Lacock

The years when Henry was pursuing his photographic research were extremely busy ones during which he juggled his intellectual interests with family life, running the Lacock estate and the public duties befitting his social position.

The 1830s was a time of great political upheaval. Many rural communities, including nearby Salisbury, witnessed violent protests, known as the Swing Riots, against the industrialisation of agriculture. Lacock was spared because the Talbot family were regarded as good landlords. However Henry's tenants were still facing poverty and, as a moderate reformer, he sought positions of political power from which he might be able improve conditions for the agricultural worker. He was elected MP for Chippenham in 1832 but retired from Parliament in 1835. He was made High Sheriff of Wiltshire, a largely ceremonial role, by Queen Victoria in 1839.

Henry became less interested in politics as he sought to spend more time on the Lacock estate with his expanding family: Ela Theresa was born in 1835, Rosamond Constance in 1837, Matilda Caroline in 1839 and his heir, Charles Henry, in 1842. The evident joy he took in family was however marred by bereavements: Captain Charles Feilding, the only father he had known, died in 1837, his beloved and inspiring mother Lady Elisabeth in 1846, and his favourite sister Horatia in 1851, ten days after the birth of her first child.

Picturing the abbey

Lacock Abbey was the first-ever building to be widely photographed and views of it, its contents and its inhabitants feature in thousands of negatives and prints. Family, friends, servants and estate workers were often requested to pose; one famous example features a group of fruit sellers and was taken in the Cloister garth. Henry's most obliging model was probably his bust of Patroclus, a hero from Greek mythology. Other still-lifes include the contents of a china cabinet in the South Gallery and the famous 'Open Door' that shows in minute detail the textures of a broom standing in William Sharington's courtyard. Another famous plate from *The Pencil of Nature* entitled 'The Ladder' was taken nearby.

Henry's legacy

Henry died in his library (now the Blue Parlour) on 17 September 1877 and is buried in the village cemetery. If he had only invented photography his life would be praiseworthy but he was also a classicist, geologist, mathematician, physicist, botanist and astronomer. He published eight books, over 100 articles and deciphered the ancient Assyrian script known as cuneiform.

In 1863 he was awarded an honorary doctorate from Edinburgh University. He felt at home in the Scottish capital, spending more and more time there so he and Constance could be near Matilda, the only one of their offspring to marry and have children. Today, the greatest memorial to Henry's achievements is Lacock itself, given to the nation by another Matilda, his granddaughter.

'I have a pleasant feeling that Lacock is rather like a tree which will go on growing, even if most of the people that sat under its shade have moved into another world.'

Matilda Talbot

Opposite above
'The Ladder', *c*.1845

Opposite below
'The Open Door', 1843

Above
'Patroclus', *c*.1841

Right 'Oak Tree in Winter', *c*.1843

The Village

With its central grid of four streets, Lacock today looks much like it did 200 years ago. Its oldest house is older than the 13th-century abbey but since the loss of the village's main source of income from wool in the 19th century, new development has been minimal.

The building materials are all local and traditional. Timber framing made from trees felled in the neighbouring forest, and weathered limestone walls and moss-encrusted stone tile roofs lend the village a harmonious unity. Almost every building is listed for its special architectural and historic interest.

Although it has more recently become famous as a film location, Lacock has had a lively and prosperous past. However it is no living museum. All the houses are lived in and the village has a vibrant community, yet the National Trust's role as landlord follows a caretaking tradition that goes all the way back to the medieval nuns of Lacock Abbey.

Origins and ownership

The name Lacock dates from Saxon times when the earliest permanent settlers lived by the Bide Brook, which runs through the middle of the village. They called it lacuc or 'little stream'.

In the Domesday Book Lacock is recorded as the property of Edward of Salisbury, Sheriff of Wiltshire, an ancestor of Ela, who founded Lacock Abbey. The medieval landscape was dominated by Melksham Forest, which came right up to the edge of the village and stretched for 33 miles to the south and east. Beside the church is a building known as King John's Hunting Lodge, where the forest's royal

owner reputedly stayed on hunting trips. Parts of the structure date from the early 1200s, making it one of Lacock's most ancient properties. Settlement began around the church, reflected in the irregular line of Church Street, but the rest is a medieval planned town, deliberately laid out on the grid of the other three streets that can still be seen today.

With the establishment of the abbey, feudal rights over the village passed to the nuns. Most of the inhabitants were 'villeins', poor tenants who paid their rent by work and goods in kind. Obligations included spreading half an acre of dung a year and helping to harvest the abbey's hay and corn before their own. Rents might be paid in corn, hides or fleeces, which, from the 14th century, were collected in the Tithe Barn on the corner of East Street and High Street. This was part of the abbey farm, its position showing just how closely the abbey and village were integrated.

Opposite Lacock's High Street

Above Traditional materials in buildings on Church Street

Left East Street, from the junction with High Street, with the 14th-century Tithe Barn just visible and the Chamberlain's House on the left

The cloth trade

Woollen cloth manufacture was a huge industry in England from the late Middle Ages to the mid-18th century. Lacock flourished over this period as it benefitted from being on the 'cloth road' that ran down Bowden Hill on its way from the West Country to London.

The abbey was a significant cloth producer and William Sharington also traded in wool. In 1242 Ela secured the right to hold a weekly Tuesday market at Lacock. The earliest market place was in front of the church, moving to High Street near the Tithe Barn around the early 1700s. The old market cross was dismantled in 1825. A version of it now stands in the school yard (see page 58).

Ela was also granted a charter to hold an annual fair in 1237 and within 20 years this had gone from being a three-day to a week-long event.

Medieval businesswomen
The Lacock nuns reared sheep on a commercial basis and had a flock of 2,000 in 1476, mostly kept at Chitterne on Salisbury Plain where abbey tenants were responsible for shearing the sheep and washing the wool. At the Dissolution of the Monasteries in 1539 Lacock Abbey had its own premises known as fulling mills, where large water-driven hammers pressed woven fabric into long bolts of cloth ready for sale.

Signs of prosperity
In 1539 Henry VIII's dissolution commissioners described Lacock Abbey as 'set in a towne'. Evidence of how the wool trade helped it flourish can still be seen in the architecture, particularly in the high number of medieval cruck frames, which suggest a concerted period of building in the 1300s and 1400s. The most impressive is the Tithe Barn where the exposed timbers rise above a floor of beaten earth. On the end wall of Cruck House on Church Street the construction of great oak curved timbers joined at the top is clearly visible but there are more than ten other hidden examples, including No. 2 High Street, which is part of a medieval terrace of houses. It can be visited on National Trust open days or rented as holiday accommodation. Dendrochronology (dating by tree rings) has shown that its main timbers were felled about 1445.

Broad looms introduced in the 15th century required wide first-floor rooms, and the banks of windows would have lit the weavers at work. The size of dwellings also bears witness to the wealth of inhabitants, like the prominent timber-framed Porch House at the entrance to the High Street and the Chamberlain's House, opposite the Tithe Barn, probably built for an abbey official.

Opposite The interior of the Tithe Barn, at one time the village's market hall

Left Porch House on High Street

Lacock church

Lacock's first church dates to the Norman occupation of the 1100s, which explains its dedication to Cyriac, a saint little known in England but more commonly remembered in the churches of Normandy. Cyriac was a three-year-old child killed by the Governor of Silicia in AD 303 for supporting the Christian faith of his martyred mother, Julitta.

The present church was largely rebuilt at the height of Lacock's prosperity, around 1450. The Lady Chapel is a couple of decades earlier and there is a small opening known as a squint between it and the north transept that gives a view of the altar. Changes over time include the addition of a 16th-century spire, the remodelling of the chancel in 1777 and again in 1903 by architect Harold Brakspear who had worked on the abbey, as well as restoration work in 1861 when the transept arches were raised to their present height.

Clear glass windows fill the interior with light giving an airy feel that is assisted by the unusually high arches pointing towards a wagon roof (so called as the closely spaced series of timbers suggest the shape of a covered wagon).

Left The interior of
St Cyriac's Church

Angels and faces

Both outside and in, the church is rich in stone carvings. In the Lady Chapel angels look down from the elaborate ceiling vault suspended between garlands of stone flowers still picked out in colour. The exterior stonework includes battlements and pinnacles along with some wonderfully characterful gargoyles. Adorning the clerestory (windows above eye level) in the north wall is a figure smoking a pipe long before the introduction of tobacco. It probably recalls the country habit of smoking dried herbs.

Family memorials

William Sharington died in 1553 but this monument is dated 1566. Its three front panels are carved with Sharington's crest and the scorpion that can be seen throughout Lacock Abbey. The cartouches (oval-shaped ornamental features containing an inscription or date) are a very early example of a type of decoration from the Netherlands, and the use of classical pilasters (rectangular columns) in an early Renaissance piece make the whole composition a fitting tribute to Sharington's advanced tastes, probably executed by his master mason John Chapman.

The chancel memorials commemorate members of the Talbot family and since 1903 the chancel has been dedicated to William Henry Fox Talbot. In the churchyard is the monument to his stepfather, Admiral Charles Feilding.

Above left Angels looking down from the ceiling of the Lady Chapel

Above St Cyriac's Church photographed c.1905

Left The sheep gate that kept animals out of the churchyard while allowing access to churchgoers

Christian charity

Lacock's nuns belonged to the Augustinian order, known for their charitable works in the wider community. Throughout the year the abbey gave a daily dole to one local destitute person. Alms were also dispensed on the anniversary of Ela's death and the deaths of her husband and father. On Maundy Thursday food and money were distributed to the needy, while 22 loaves of bread were given out on Good Friday.

Lacock opens up

Lacock continued as a prosperous community of craftsmen throughout the 1500s and 1600s. With the sale and destruction of Melksham Forest from 1618 it lost its woodland barrier and roads began to improve. The London to Bath road became a toll road in 1713 helping to finance improvements including the 18th-century packhorse bridge over the Bide Brook.

Tudor and Jacobean houses along West Street testify to the skills of Lacock builders but the 18th century saw the introduction of red brick. The elegant Cantax House, built about 1700, had an on-site workshop for finishing cloth. It became the vicarage from around 1760 to 1866. The Red Lion pub was entirely rebuilt in 1722, but is only red on the front because bricks were too expensive to use for the whole structure.

Inns and incarceration

Lacock has four public houses – in 1620 there were seven alehouses – and, next to the Tithe Barn, an 18th-century stone blind-house of a distinctive Wiltshire type, where drunkards were locked up overnight. The George in West Street holds one of the longest continuous licences in the West Country, reputedly first licensed in 1361, having been known simply as The Inn before it was remodelled and renamed during the reign of George II. Its open fire

Right The 18th-century packhorse bridge brought increased trade to Lacock

1800s. In his role as MP, William Henry Fox Talbot petitioned Parliament to assist the village, where some 200 people were unemployed in 1833. A lucky few received sponsorship and emigrated to Canada. The less fortunate ended up in the village poorhouse on the corner of the lane by the church. This was replaced by the new workhouse (now a pottery and B&B) in 1833.

Next to the former workhouse is the early 1800s bark-drying shed of the tanyard, where leather was made. The proximity of these buildings is no coincidence as workhouse inmates were employed in the thriving tannery to do the exceedingly dirty and smelly work of preparing animals skins in the tanning pits or vats. Bark from local oak and ash trees, which contains the substance tannin, was mixed with water in which the skins were soaked. The large openings under the eaves of the drying shed once had slats to control ventilation and aid drying.

retains the wheel of a 17th-century turnspit used for roasting and originally powered by a dog. On Church Street, The Angel is a purpose-built inn of around 1480, named after a gold coin rather than the heavenly messenger.

Harsh realities

From the early 1800s onwards the Industrial Revolution brought hard times for Lacock, as the handlooms traditionally used by West Country weavers were superseded by mechanical looms in factories. The Berkshire and Wiltshire Canal, opened in 1810, linked Lacock into the national transport network. When William Henry Fox Talbot rejected a bid by Isambard Kingdom Brunel to bring the Chippenham to Weymouth railway to within a mile of the abbey, modernisation of the village ceased.

The fact that there have been so few modern alterations in Lacock as a whole is partly due to ownership by a single landlord but also reflects its dependence on wool wealth, which had evaporated by the early

Left The blind-house (it has no windows) was used to hold village drunks until they sobered up

Below The Sign of the Angel in 1905 with a horse passage that led to stables behind the pub

Life in a rural community

Lacock village, whether in times of prosperity or recession, and long before it became fashionable, has been a community that looks locally for its needs. Whether wood, wool or water, its wealth of resources helped the village to remain largely self-sufficient until the 1970s.

Lacock already had a school when William Henry Fox Talbot inherited the estate but his love of education inspired him to establish a new one. Dated 1824 with extensions in 1852 and 1869, it is in the Tudor Revival style he used at the abbey. Pupil numbers peaked at 120, and between 1879 and 1972 there were just three headmasters. It is still a thriving school today.

'Haymaking is interfering with the attendance just now. Several children are allowed to go out earlier than usual to take tea to their fathers in the hayfield.'

School logbook, July 1902

Cottage industry

In 1903 Lacock had 18 local businesses. There were four grocers and four bakers, two butchers, two blacksmiths – one at the forge, which is now a bus shelter on West Street – a 'fancy goods' store, draper and tailor. Mrs Butler's Coffee Tavern at No. 2 High Street was renowned for its generous portions of bread pudding and cake. Craftsmen included two builders – one a carpenter and undertaker, the other a mason – a hurdle maker, plumbers and chairmakers. The postmaster from 1927–66 was called Harry Potter. He worked six days a week from the post office at No. 19 High Street, the building with the clock on its door. This clock is in fact double-faced, with the same time showing on the inside, presumably to avoid after-hours arguments about missed post (see back cover).

No. 2 High Street became the Post Office in 1966, run by Miss Peggy Butler. It closed in the early 1980s but much of the shop stock and Miss Butler's collection of bygones displayed in the window remains in it. Old shop windows tell the story of retail past and present: the National Trust shop in a building of around 1600 has an original fireplace and an early to mid-1800s shop window.

Opposite The school was built to accommodate 100 pupils of all ages and the Talbot coat of arms is on the wall of the original building; photographed c.1905

Left The Old Post Office at No. 19 High Street

Below left Lacock's bakery

20th-century changes

Matilda Talbot took her role as village landlord seriously and was loved as a result. When she decided to sell valuable books, pictures and tapestries from the abbey it was for the benefit of her tenants. In 1918 she funded cottage repairs and in 1936 paid for the installation of indoor lavatories. Her decision to give Lacock to the National Trust in 1944 ensured its historic integrity, protecting it from the commercial pressures that have distorted other pretty villages. The old English way of life once exemplified by Lacock may be a thing of the past but it retains a vital and vibrant community.

The Lacock Pageant

In 1932 the 700th anniversary of Lacock Abbey was celebrated in a village-wide pageant. Matilda Talbot played the foundress Ela and the Bishop of Southampton performed the blessing. The 13th-century backdrop was created by costumed villagers who became medieval versions of themselves, and Lacock's blacksmith built a forge copied from a manuscript in the British Museum. A day of dancing, singing and feasting was enjoyed by 10,000 people. It was repeated in 1933 and a film of it can be seen in the abbey.

Lacock on Screen

The village has hosted many film crews in need of an historic backdrop. From Robin Hood and Jane Austen to the fantasy settings of Harry Potter's Hogwarts, Lacock has so often graced screens large and small that it is not surprising if visitors sometimes feel a sense of déjà vu.

Lacock becomes Cranford

To a great many who have never even visited Lacock, its streets, houses and shop fronts are strikingly familiar. For two weeks in April 2007 Lacock was transformed into the small Cheshire market town invented by Elizabeth Gaskell and became, for millions of viewers, the eponymous location of 'Cranford'.

The fact that Lacock's streets are largely free of modern-day intrusions makes it understandably popular with location directors: there are no television aerials, satellite dishes and such that would have to be removed or disguised for costume dramas.

For the making of 'Cranford', an army of set designers turned the clock back to the 1840s, spreading earth over the Tarmac, dressing front windows and giving the Red Lion a false shop front which allowed locals to walk through Johnson's store into the pub behind.

With an all-star cast led by Dame Judi Dench, the BBC series found worldwide success with its depiction of a community on the cusp of change. The coming of the railways had a profound effect on towns and villages across Britain and Lacock's own story would have been very different if the railway had arrived on its doorstep instead of bypassing it.

Opposite Lacock is transformed for the filming of BBC period drama 'Cranford'

Above left False snow being sprayed one June evening in Lacock for the Christmas edition of 'Cranford'

Above Market day in Cranford

Movie magic at Lacock

The world of Harry Potter as filmed by Warner Brothers is a magical mix of locations from all over Britain. Lacock Abbey contributed some of Hogwarts' rooms for *The Philosopher's Stone* (2001) and *The Chamber of Secrets* (2002). The Cloister appeared in the Mrs Norris cat scenes, Professor Snape's laboratory was filmed in the Sacristy and the nuns' Warming House became the classroom of Harry and his friends.

Jane Austen's *Pride and Prejudice* has twice been filmed at Lacock, first in 1967 and again in 1995 for the BBC production starring Colin Firth as the aloof and brooding Mr Darcy. In 1996 Austen came to Lacock again for a film adaptation of *Emma* in which the heroine was played by Kate Beckinsale. Daniel Defoe's *Moll Flanders* saw Lacock revert to the 1600s in the same year. The abbey and village have been used for two Thomas Hardy adaptations:

Above Filming of *The Other Boleyn Girl* in the Cloister

The Mayor of Casterbridge in 2003 and *Tess of the d'Urbervilles* in 2008.

In the early 1980s Robin Hood and his band of outlaws were regular visitors to the village and abbey for episodes of the ITV series 'Robin of Sherwood', in which the lead was played first by Michael Praed and then by Jason Connery.

Lacock has more recently hosted Hollywood stars with the filming in 2008 of *The Other Boleyn Girl* starring Natalie Portman, Scarlett Johansson and Eric Bana.

Left A scene from *The Mayor of Casterbridge* in the Stable Court

Below The Chapter House dressed for a scene in *The Other Boleyn Girl*

All Lacock's visitors

Today the National Trust follows a long tradition of welcoming visitors to Lacock that goes back to the 13th-century hospitality of Ela and her nuns.

Modern-day visitors walk in the footsteps of medieval wool traders, Tudor courtiers, Civil War soldiers, Georgian garden designers and Victorian scientists. After the abbey passed into private hands at the Dissolution, no lesser person than Queen Elizabeth I visited, repaying her host Henry Sharington with a knighthood.

It is nearly 800 years since the foundation of Lacock Abbey. Ten thousand people came to the 700th-anniversary pageant organised by Matilda Talbot in 1932. Her family's ownership of the abbey and estate began in 1540 and came to an end when she made a gift of Lacock to the National Trust in 1944. That continuity and family tradition have been important in preserving the abbey and village, but there has been innovation too, in the way in which the buildings have responded to architectural fashions and, most notably, in William Henry Fox Talbot's world-changing invention of photography.

Since the conversion to holiday accommodation of the 14th-century house and former coffee tavern at No. 2 High Street, anyone can follow the royal example and stay at Lacock. With a strong local community in the village and a dedicated staff looking after the 325-acre estate, it continues to be a lively place, where the past remains wonderfully present.

Below Hospitality and a warm welcome are as much a feature of Lacock as they ever were